MY ALABAMA DISABILITY CLAIM

A Guide to Your Alabama Workers' Compensation and Social Security Case

WILLIAM **POWELL**
& GREGORY **DENNY**

Published by Legal Pro Books

My Alabama Disability Claim

ISBN: 0615484786
ISBN-13: 9780615484785

Published by Legal Pro Books USA

www.powellanddenny.com

Table of Contents

Part Three: Why I May Need a Lawyer Who Does Workers' Compensation and Social Security

Part Four: Disability Odds and Ends

Part Five: About the Authors

Read This First

This book is intended as an introduction to the subject of social security disability claims and workers' compensation claims in the state of Alabama. It is our intent to be as helpful as possible, but we must point out that it is not a legal treatise. While we hope that our readers find it informative, it is important to remember that other jurisdictions have laws, rules and practices that may be different from those discussed here. Also, laws change frequently, and one should not use this book as a substitute for legal advice on any matter. This book is not intended to give legal advice on specific cases, nor does the sale or transfer of this book constitute an entrance into an attorney-client relationship.

As this book notes, the practice of these areas of the law can be confusing and complicated. Each person who obtains this book should consult an attorney before making legal decisions and should not rely on this book in order to handle any aspect of their claim. To the extent this book could be construed as advertisement we have included the following: "No representation is made that the quality of the legal services to be performed is greater than the quality of legal services performed by other lawyers."

Introduction

My Workers' Compensation and Social Security Case

This book was written with the injured/disabled person in mind. We chose the title and the theme of this book because this is *your case*. No matter how good a lawyer you hire, your injuries and disabilities are your own, and you are the one who has to live with them. If you decide to hire a lawyer, you should find a lawyer who keeps this in mind. Much of this book will discuss what we know about Alabama workers' compensation and social security cases, but even though this book tells you a lot about us, and we have both handled thousands of these types of cases, we are not the ones who are injured. There is a good chance that, if you are reading this book, either you or a family member is currently disabled and making a claim. At our firm, the way we look at it is that we're helping you with *your claim*. We hope that spirit comes through, because this book was written to help *you* understand *your claim*. And while your claim may be only a workers' compensation claim or only a social security claim, we hope to show you how hiring a lawyer who does *both* social security and workers' compensation can be an advantage to winning either type of claim you have.

Meeting with a Disability Lawyer

Most people meet with a lawyer maybe once or twice in their entire lives. When you meet with a lawyer on a case where you are no longer able to work, you should expect to meet with someone who is knowledgeable about disability claims. Two of the most common types of disability claims are workers' compensation claims and social security claims. At our law firm here in Alabama, we do only those types of cases that relate to workers' compensation or social security. We focus on these two types of cases because they are similar. Most people who come in for either type of case have a lot of things in common:

1. They are use to working.
2. They can no longer work and are disabled, either temporarily or permanently.
3. They are worried about how they are going to pay their bills.
4. They are worried about what will happen if they lose their case and they are still unable to work.
5. They are worried about long-term medical treatment for their injury or disease.

Whether they were hurt at work and will be off six months for surgery, or they have a serious disease and will never work again, the concerns are often the same. Both situations are very stressful, and you want to be able to count on either a workers' compensation settlement or a social security check to help you through these tough times.

At our law firm, we handle both workers' compensation and social security cases for a reason. Both of these cases involve the inability to work, and knowledge of all the rules in one area can help you dramatically with your case in the other. Many lawyers do either one or the other; some lawyers handle only a few such cases. Our firm has handled thousands of each. Because of this, we have learned a lot about the reasons people cannot work. We also have learned that, while the two areas are related, they are not exactly the same. The standards are different, and the laws are different. Understanding both the differences and the similarities and knowing how to use them to our clients' advantage is what makes our law firm different.

At our firm, we believe you should expect to meet with the attorney who is actually going to handle your case. This is very important, because you do not want to be meeting the lawyer who will handle the most important case of your life five minutes before court. Unfortunately, at other firms, many people do not meet with their attorneys until it is very late into their case. This can cause many problems in preparing for your hearing or trial. It also can make you very uncomfortable, because your lawyer is essentially a stranger.

Your lawyer should not be a stranger. You should expect that your lawyer will take the time to listen to what you have to say about the history of your injury or illness.

Below is a list that will give you an idea of the questions you should be prepared to discuss when you first call.

1. Name
2. Date of injury or illness
3. Years you have worked
4. Who you have worked for
5. Your educational history
6. The doctors you have seen
7. The severity of your problems
8. How long you think you will be off work
9. Prior disability claims or injuries

You should also expect to get an idea of what is going to happen on your case in some detail. The rest of this book is a summarized version of some of the main things you would learn if you meet with us in person. It is our sincere hope that this will give you an idea of what to expect in the long, tough process of filing for benefits when you have become disabled and unable to provide for yourself and your family.

Regardless of the difficulty of these cases, one thing you should most definitely expect is that your lawyer is on your side and is not another enemy in the process. You and your attorney should work together in this time of great difficulty. At our firm, we came up with a phrase to express how we feel about this:

Powell and Denny: We Work When You Can't.

How Does My Attorney Get Paid?

One of the primary concerns, if not *the* primary concern, that people have when they meet with a lawyer is how they are going to pay the lawyer. Most people are concerned that there will be a hidden cost or that they are going to be treated unfairly. At our firm, we provide our prospective client with a short, one-page, easy-to-read contract that makes it clear: We Don't Get Paid Unless You Do. Furthermore, there are no charges for coming in to have us evaluate your case. While some attorneys do charge for initial evaluations of claims, we do not. Fees in most workers' compensation and social security claims in Alabama are handled on a contingency basis, which means the fee is collected out of what we win on your claim. The fee in Alabama for workers comp is 15% of the recovery. The fee on social security is 25% of the back benefits check. You also will have to pay expenses, in most cases. Our firm charges expenses only in the event we win your case, but one should be aware that some firms charge for expenses even if the case is lost.

While this is obviously one of the most important aspects of the claim from the perspective of both the client and the lawyer, it is not as important as having a good relationship with one another. If a client and lawyer have a good relationship, the fee is almost never an issue. Especially given the fact that fees are often much higher in other types of cases; for instance, fees in car accident cases typically run from 30% to 50% of the recovery. Unlike those types of cases, state and federal laws restrict what lawyers can charge in Alabama workers' compensation and social security matters. And in both these cases, a judge almost always must approve the fee. For this reason, more protection is afforded to workers' compensation and social security clients than in most other areas of the law.

Part One: My Alabama Workers' Compensation Injury

Introduction to Alabama's Workers' Compensation Law

When we first meet with prospective clients and explain the limitations incorporated in Alabama's Workers' Compensation Statute, most people are not pleased with the law, but after providing a very brief history of the workers' compensation system, most people have a better appreciation for both the benefits of, and problems with, workers' compensation laws.

Workers' compensation claims are not like other personal injury claims. In most personal injury claims, a person can ask a jury for money to cover a multitude of things, including pain and suffering. For the most part, these damages are not available to Alabama workers who are injured while performing their job duties. As will be discussed later, workers injured in Alabama are restricted to recovery based upon the Alabama Workers' Compensation Statute.

From ancient times to the present, the legal system has created a means for injured parties to be paid if they were injured due to the fault of another, but the party that was supposedly at fault was also allowed to make arguments to defeat these claims. In many cases, these defenses prevented those injured or killed on the job from any form of recovery. For example, if a worker worked with explosives, he was often prevented from suing his employer if a piece of dynamite prematurely exploded and seriously injured him, because his job inherently involved a high degree of risk, of which he was aware when he agreed to work there. If a worker took a wrong step and slipped and fell off a ladder, he was partially at fault and therefore unable to seek any money for his injury and time off work. Many countries and states began making laws to make the system fairer. Workers' compensation came about so that employers, who were financially better off than their workers, would bear the burden of paying for most job injuries. In return, they were given certain protections, which kept them from being pursued for the full damages an injured employee might incur. In other words, almost everyone who is hurt gets covered, but what they can recover is limited by law.

In the 1920s, Alabama became one of the last States to adopt a workers' compensation statute. In a nutshell, Alabama's Workers' Compensation Statute gets rid of the idea of fault in job-related injuries and instead approaches the injury in a no-fault manner. Now, instead of an injured worker having to prove that his employer caused the accident (and showing that he was totally blame free), a worker has to show is that he suffered a work-related injury while performing his job duties and that timely notice of said injury was provided to his employer. In Alabama, if a worker can show this, then generally his employer must pay for all of the worker's reasonably necessary medical treatment and reimburse the worker for mileage in driving back and forth for medical treatment. They also pay the worker 2/3rds of his or her average weekly wage when the worker is held off work by a workers' compensation doctor treating him for job injuries. These payments typically last until the date the doctor says that the worker has reached maximum medical improvement. The employer also pays the injured worker for any permanent physical disability sustained as a result of an on-the-job injury. In exchange for forcing the employer to pay when an employee is injured, the injured worker gives up certain rights and benefits—including the right to compensation for pain and suffering.

So, while a worker in Alabama who suffers a job-related injury is limited by law in what he or she can receive in a workers' compensation claim, what workers now are legally entitled to is, on the whole, much better than what was available prior to our workers' compensation laws.

Do I Have a Workers' Compensation Claim?

In Alabama, for an injured worker to have a workers' compensation claim, several hurdles have to be cleared. First, the injured worker must actually be an employee of the defendant. While this may sound simple, at times huge battles erupt between defendants over who actually employed an injured worker. As a rule of thumb, whoever directs you in when and how you perform your job duties will be considered your employer, although at times this is not true.

Second, your employer must be subject to Alabama's workers' compensation laws. In Alabama, an employer has to have five (5) or more employees regularly employed to fall under our workers' compensation system. Employees of the state of Alabama must seek compensation through another system set up for state employees

Third, you must show that you suffered an on-the-job injury while performing your job duties for your employer. Injuries caused by a worker goofing off or engaging in horse play or injuries caused by the worker being under the influence of alcohol and/or drugs are not considered injuries sustained while performing your job duties and are not covered. However, since Alabama's workers' compensation laws are no-fault in nature, the fact that the injured worker accidentally contributed to his injury does not prevent him from seeking and receiving workers' compensation benefits. For example, if a worker is not paying attention to where he is and falls off a ledge, he usually is not prohibited from receiving workers' compensation benefits even though the accident was his fault; however, if the worker fell off a ledge due to being intoxicated, that is another matter.

Fourth, the injured worker has an obligation to inform his employer that he has suffered a work-related injury. Often, workers are not sure whether they have suffered a serious injury or just a sprain, so they do not report anything until later. We have spoken to numerous people who call our office after being told by their employers that they have waited too long to report a job injury and therefore are not entitled to any workers' compensation benefits. This is rarely true and is sometimes an intentional lie. In Alabama, a worker has up to 90 days in which to inform his employer about a job injury, and a verbal report is valid. Having stated this, *it is always best to report a potential job injury as soon as possible.*

Lastly, the injured worker has to show that the injury he is complaining about was the result of the job accident he suffered. This can be a difficult thing to show. If a worker falls off a scaffold, landing in front of his boss and suffering a fracture, showing that the job accident led to the fracture is usually simple. What may be difficult is showing that the fall also caused the worker to suffer a neck injury—especially if the worker had a history of neck pain. This leads us to a different but related issue: a pre-existing condition.

We could not count the number of times we have had a client come into our office who was injured at work but was informed that workers' comp was refusing to accept liability because, 20 years earlier, the worker had hurt the same body part while playing high school baseball or in an automobile accident. This argument rarely works for the employer. In Alabama, if a worker has a pre-existing condition that has not stopped them from being able to adequately perform their job duties, the law views the condition as being irrelevant. If you can do your job duties and a job accident worsens an underlying condition, then workers' compensation has to pick up your claim for the worsened condition. We have had discussions with insurance adjusters such as the one in which the adjuster attempted to explain that our client's leg injury was really related to the fracture he suffered playing high school football and not due to the fall from a roof top he suffered at work. If you hear this "defense" from an insurance adjuster, you are most likely being given the run-around, and it is time to get a lawyer, if you have not already done so.

Alabama's Workers' Compensation System: What to Expect

Unfortunately, having a workers' compensation claim is often confusing and frustrating. The injured worker believes that—having suffered a job injury—comp will do what they are supposed to do and take care of his medical treatment and ensure that he receives his workers' compensation check on time. The insurance carriers do not always see it this way; too often they act as though their job is to ensure you receive the least amount of medical attention and compensation possible.

First, as soon as possible, the injured worker needs to inform his boss and employer of the job injury he has suffered. At this point, general information is taken down, and usually the worker is asked if he needs to see a doctor. Many times the injured employee will say, "No, let's just see if it will work itself out." While this sentiment may seem noble, it rarely works to the injured worker's advantage. More times than not, this refusal of medical treatment is used by the insurance company down the line as evidence that the injury could not have been very serious because the employee didn't think much of it immediately afterwards. If you have suffered an injury serious enough to report, you probably have suffered an injury serious enough to have a doctor look at it.

Usually after a worker reports a job injury, he will receive two things. First, he will receive a phone call from an adjuster who informs him that his workers' compensation insurance company is investigating his alleged job injury, and second, he will receive a request for a recorded statement. The adjuster says the recording is needed to assist them in their investigation, but what they are doing is getting the injured worker nailed down as to every facet of their case—how the injury occurred, any pre-existing problems and what problems the person is now having. An example of what routinely happens is that a worker reports a job accident to his employer and then is sent to the company doctor and receives pain medication. Later that evening, the worker receives a call from the insurance carrier, who asks to take a recorded statement. In the statement, the worker, who was caught off guard and is in pain and feeling the side effects of his pain pills, neglects to mention one or two important facts. Down the road, the worker can rest assured that the insurance carrier will use the recorded statement in an attempt to escape liability. This is why they are calling you—so they can get some ammunition to use against you later.

The next day, the injured worker might awake to find a medical release in his or her mail box. The insurance company has mailed this to the worker and wants him to sign it so they can get *all* of his medical records. When we say *all*, we mean *all* of them. We have had cases where the insurance carrier had records from when the worker was a child. The insurance company is prepared to spend hundreds of dollars at the onset of your claim in an attempt to get out of liability, and let there be no doubt that that is the reason why they want your medical records. The insurance carrier is hoping that, in your past, you have suffered an injury to the same body part, and based on that, they can deny liability; even better, they are hoping that you suffered an injury to this body part in the past and forgot to mention this to them when they took your statement, so they can twist this into claiming you are dishonest.

During the course of your medical treatment, you will be asked to see the doctor workers' compensation tells you to see. While you are free to see any doctor you wish, in order for workers' compensation to pay for your medical treatment, you do have to see their doctor, and if you try to use your health insurance on a comp claim, your insurance carrier will not pay if the workers' compensation insurance carrier is supposed to. So, in essence, you have to see whoever the workers' compensation insurance adjuster sends you to see. In seeing the doctor, be sure to inform her of all symptoms and pains you are having and then mention them again during every visit. While most physicians are of the highest quality, there are some who make a substantial amount of money treating injured workers, and some of these doctors seem to go out of their way to hurt a workers' claim. At our firm, we try to steer out clients away from these doctors to ensure that our clients receive the medical treatment they require in a timely manner.

While seeing the company physician, you may be given physical restrictions. Your employer can find a job that falls within your limitations or create one for you. If a job is available, our advice is to go to work and do your best, regardless of whether you believe you can do the job. If the job aggravates your condition, let your employer and physician know so changes can be made. We are always envisioning our clients and ourselves standing before a judge in the not-too-distant future, and we want our client to be able to say that he did everything that was asked of him—even though it caused him some discomfort.

It is possible that, during the course of your medical treatment, you will be contacted by someone who represents herself as a case nurse manager. She may or may not tell you that she works for the insurance carrier, but she will be sure to tell you that her job is to help you. Unfortunately, with a few rare exceptions, her job is not to help you but to convince your treating physician to release you back to work as quickly as possible, regardless of your condition or pain. Be on guard in terms of what you talk to this case nurse manager about, and under no circumstances should you allow her to be in the examination room when the doctor meets with you. That is the time for you and the doctor to discuss your case and for her to answer your questions and concerns—not those of the insurance company.

If your employer cannot, or will not, accommodate your restrictions or if a physician takes you off work, you will become entitled to temporary total disability (TTD) benefits. TTD benefits are only 66% of your average weekly wage. Your average weekly wage is calculated by averaging your wages for the 52-week period immediately preceding your job injury. The calculation of your average weekly wage is supposed to include any bonuses you received in the year prior to your job injury and does not include any week in which you did not earn any money or use vacation time. These details are routinely forgotten by the adjuster in calculating your average weekly wage. You also need to bring them to your lawyers attention as well.

You will be entitled to TTD benefits until your employer finds a job for you or until you reach maximum medical improvement (MMI). Maximum medical improvement is the date on which your treating physician believes you have recovered as much as possible following your injury. Once you reach MMI, your right to TTD benefits stops. At this time, the doctor should state whether you have suffered any permanent physical impairment or whether you now have any permanent restrictions.

During the course of your medical treatment, you may become dissatisfied with your treating physician. In Alabama, the law does allow you to choose a new physician from a list of four doctors provided by the workers' comp insurance carrier. Usually you have the right to make this change only once during your case, so this is not a decision to be made on the spur of the moment. Great thought should be given prior to requesting a panel of four physicians; if you have decided to make a change, the advice of an attorney is invaluable, as attorneys who handle a lot of workers' compensation claims will be in the best position to advise you on whom to choose given your medical problems.

It is also important to remember, whenever you are in public, you are subject to being videotaped. Some insurance carriers rarely use surveillance, while others almost always hire someone to follow the injured worker around in hopes of seeing him do something he is not supposed to do, or so they can take it to the treating physician to compare what the injured worker says he can do, with what the video shows. There is no law against someone videotaping you in a public place, and we always tell our clients that if they are honest and forthright with us and the doctor, there really isn't anything to worry about. Having stated this, we have seen examples where six months of videotape has been edited into 20 minutes of potentially damaging footage. That is why, when we meet with our clients or prepare them for depositions, we ask them to think about how they feel over the course of a week. You have good days, bad days and average days. Injured workers need to keep this in mind when talking with their treating physicians and when giving their depositions. Every day is not the worst day, and on good days they try their best to have a normal life. Presenting your case this way will help your credibility with the doctors and judges and could help the value of your case.

The vast majority of workers' compensation claims settle because they should. Even if suit has to be filed, chances are that the case will settle, but you cannot assume your case will settle. You are not entitled to a settlement; the insurance carrier cannot be forced to pay you anything unless a judge orders them to do so, and sometimes these cases have to go to trial. When we file suit in our firm, we view the case as one that we will have to try and work hard to prepare the case and our client for trial. This preparation generally helps the case settle, as our clients know what to expect and present themselves and their case in a reasonable manner, which can cause an insurance carrier to reassess the amount of money they are willing to pay to settle a claim. More than a few times, we have settled cases based on the defendant saying that they like and believe our client and that they feared that the judge would, as well.

In those situations where suit has to be filed, you should be aware that nothing happens overnight. Once suit is filed, the defendant (your employer) has to be served with a copy of the suit, and sometimes this can take several weeks. The defendant has 30 days in which to file their response, and then both sides will engage in discovery—in which each side asks the other side questions, requests certain documents and takes depositions. Once discovery is filed, both sides have 30 days in which to respond to the other's requests, and arguments about some responses may have to be taken before the judge. Eventually, the defense attorney will want to take your deposition. Client preparation is vitally important at this phase.

We tell our clients to assume that the defense attorney knows absolutely everything about them. They know about every legal problem you have ever had. They know if you have ever been forced to file for bankruptcy protection and whether your case was dismissed. They know the status of your child support payments. They know about any other lawsuits you have ever been involved in or whether you have ever made a claim for workers' compensation benefits before this claim. We tell our clients to assume that the defense attorney knows everything about them and their case, and that they already know the answer to every question they are asking. Why, then, the need for the deposition, you may ask. The primary reason is to determine if you are honest and likeable. Remember, you are the greatest strength in your claim, but you can also be the biggest weakness.

We have found that in most cases where our clients have not told the truth, they were not doing so in an attempt to make their case better, but rather because they were embarrassed about something in their past. However, this is not an excuse for lying once you are placed under oath. We use the following examples in preparing our clients for their depositions:

We had a client with a serious injury; the insurance company doubted whether our client had actually sustained his injury at work or elsewhere, so they denied liability. In preparing our client for his deposition, it became apparent that he was lying about past drug use. We explained to our client that there was absolutely no evidence that he was on drugs at the time of his job accident, or that drugs could have caused his accident, so there was no reason to worry about the past drug use unless he lied about it. Our client did not listen to us and lied about his past drug use during his deposition, and at trial this became apparent. The judge ruled against us, and our client received nothing.

We had another client who had been convicted of a serious crime in the past and had spent years in prison. We explained to our client that the defendant already knew about it and that the crime would not be an issue at trial unless he lied. Our client told the truth and ended up with a very good settlement.

The client who received everything he was entitled to had a serious criminal conviction in his past, while the client who was never even so much as arrested, received nothing. The reason? One was honest, while the other tried to lie.

Always tell the truth; the defendant and judge will usually know if you are lying.

Prior to trial, both sides will attempt to reach a settlement. You should know that, in Alabama, if you try your case, the judge cannot order the defendant to make a lump sum payment to you. The judge will decide whether you have suffered a job injury; if so, the judge will rule on the extent of your permanent impairment and/or loss of use, and the insurance carrier will have the option of paying you weekly for the time specified in Alabama's Workers' Compensation Statute. During settlement discussions, your attorney will attempt to obtain the largest lump sum payment he or she can on your behalf. If the amount is not sufficient, you are free to take the matter before the court, but you will probably not be paid a lump sum amount.

If settlement is not possible in your case, you will need extensive preparation for the testimony you will offer at trial. At our firm, we meet several times with our clients, and we perform cross-examinations to prepare our client for the worst-case scenario. This process is not fun for our clients, but it is necessary. We review everything with our clients, from your sworn deposition testimony and your medical history to what to wear at trial. When you are taking your case before a judge, nothing should be left to chance. Your testimony will probably last 60–90 minutes; to be properly prepared to testify for this length of time, you may need several hours of prep time. You should be nervous but not scared. If you are properly prepared, you will not be frightened.

If it is determined that you suffered a compensable on-the-job injury, the workers' compensation insurance carrier has to pay for all reasonable and necessary medical treatment for the rest of your life. It is important to note, however, that they are responsible only as long as the treatment is related specifically to your job injury. If, after your settlement or trial, you suffer another injury to the body part, workers' compensation will most likely no longer be responsible for paying for your medical treatment, as that responsibility now belongs to another party.

Clients understandably believe that once their case has been litigated and the judge has made a favorable decision, the case is over, but this is not necessarily true. The defendant has a right to appeal the decision first to the Alabama Court of Civil Appeals and then to the Alabama Supreme Court, if their initial appeal is unsuccessful. An experienced attorney will not only help you win your case at trial, but will ensure that all the appropriate evidence is submitted to the trial court and preserved for appeal purposes.

An Important Warning Regarding the Internet

In the past few years, email, instant messaging, Facebook, Myspace and Twitter have changed the way people interact with each other. Many people routinely place photos of themselves on their sites and discuss what is happening in their lives. You should be aware that information posted on such sites may be discoverable by the insurance carrier's attorneys, and they will take the time to find these sites. Anything posted on these sites can be used against you in court. Furthermore, if you post the details of any discussions held between yourself and your attorney, you may be found to have waived your right to attorney-client privilege. It is also a good idea to avoid writing emails to the insurance adjuster or case manager. *Many lawyers for insurance companies start researching you online the moment they get a file or when the insurance carrier sends them loads of emails that you have written to the insurance adjuster. This can cause tremendous problems for your case.*

What Is My Workers' Compensation Case Worth?

This is a more complicated question than most people realize. In order to answer the question, one must be able to determine a worker's degree of disability. For example, a person who has no lingering effects from an injury and goes back to work making the same money and working the same hours he did before the injury may be entitled to no settlement at all. On the other hand, a person with several surgeries and numerous restrictions may be entitled to hundreds of thousands of dollars. But in order to evaluate either case, one must know the degree of disability, and this is something that is typically not known until the end of medical treatment and even then is usually a matter of great dispute.

Usually one of the worst ways to judge the value of your comp case is by listening to family and friends' stories about how a friend of a friend got X amount of dollars for an injury just like yours. Workers' compensation cases are very unusual in that they fall under a specialized area of the law. The amount of money paid in a compensation case is based on factors that are radically different from those in any other kind of case. There are a number of caps and deductions that are part of the law that limit an injured worker's recovery. Just as important, there are a number of ways to calculate the amount that is owed in a workers' compensation case. For these reasons, it is very difficult to determine how much a worker should be paid; sometimes this is not even easy for an attorney with years of experience. A worker without representation is at a huge disadvantage when he or she is negotiating a settlement based on these calculations.

Insurance adjusters know that there are various ways to make these calculations, so what they typically do is use the most conservative method and present it to the unrepresented worker as the calculation that they are entitled to under law. While this is technically true, the adjuster will not tell you that another calculation may be much higher and also may be what you are entitled to under law.

In short, about the only chance you have of getting a reliably accurate calculation of your claim is go to a lawyer you trust and provide that lawyer with all the available information on your claim. Even in these circumstances, there may be more than one answer to this important question.

Why I May Need an Attorney

Throughout the section dealing with workers' compensation claims in Alabama, we have set forth some of the issues you will face. We have had several trials where the main issue of contention was who actually employed the injured worker, so you can see that even what appears to be a simple issue can turn out to be rather complex. The vast majority of injured workers do not have the faintest idea how to properly present their case, and this can be very costly. The difference in a worker being 99% vocationally disabled and 100% vocationally disabled can easily be a difference of $100,000.00. If a doctor's deposition needs to be taken, an experienced attorney is invaluable, as your case can hinge on a few words. It is not unusual for a client to hire our firm after being offered a settlement by workers' compensation. The insurance carrier has informed them that they are offering the value of their case and that hiring an attorney would be pointless. Usually this is not the case, and most times our clients receive more money even after our fee and expenses are deducted. On more than one occasion, people have walked into our office with offers to settle and have left our offices later with settlements that were double or triple that original offer.

If you think your injury may have left you totally disabled, hiring an attorney who handles both workers' compensation claims and social security disability claims is a must. This is discussed in more detail in "Part Three: Why I May Need a Lawyer Who Does Workers' Compensation and Social Security."

Lastly, while we have attempted to briefly discuss many issues you will face during your workers' compensation claim, not all issues are appropriate in this form, as they can be extremely difficult to explain in a concise manner.

In Alabama, no one has to hire an attorney to represent his or her interest in a workers' compensation claim, but you can rest assured that the insurance company will have their attorneys working to protect their interest. It just makes sense to level the playing field.

Part Two: My Alabama Social Security Claim

Why Was My Claim Denied?

Most people who call us or come into our offices are upset when they first contact us. They are upset because they have received a letter from the Social Security Administration that explains to them the reasons the Administration says they are not disabled. Usually, these letters are rather vague and explain that, while the Administration has determined that you are injured or ill, you are not, in their opinion, disabled.

Our prospective clients are relieved to know that, in most cases, the turn down is just a form letter and most of what the letter contains was not written with them specifically in mind. After a few moments, the person is usually angered again when they realize that the letter they received, which denied them their much needed benefits, was just a form letter. At this point we explain that a larger percentage of people who are approved are approved only after they appeal their case and request a hearing.

At our firm, we attempt to win the case prior to a hearing by making special requests for favorable decisions based on evidence we compile with the client's assistance. Despite our efforts, a large number of people are going to end up going to a hearing, and that is really their best opportunity to win their case.

Although you might have a very good case on paper, winning a case often requires sitting before a person who has the power to order your benefits paid. While this may seem daunting to someone who has never appeared in court before, these hearings are actually relatively informal, and they are the one opportunity you have to tell a flesh and blood person the reasons you are disabled. The fact that your claim was denied upon the initial application is not a reason to think that you should not pursue your claim further. Many people have walked into our law offices depressed and discouraged and eventually left a courtroom where a judge had just awarded them their benefits.

In short, the reasons why a case is turned down are often not easy to discover because they usually come to you in the form of a vague letter. The one thing you should trust is your own opinion regarding your ability to engage in work. If you feel certain your physical or mental condition will keep you from working, you should take your denial letter to a lawyer for an expert analysis of your claim. An attorney who has handled hundreds of claims will be able to tell you the pros and cons of your particular case.

What to Do When My Claim Is Denied

When your application for benefits is denied, you have only a short time period in which you can appeal your claim. Most people should consult an attorney as soon as they are turned down so they can make a decision about how to handle any appeal. Many people simply give up on their claim. They don't realize that this is really the point at which the actual road to winning their case begins.

The biggest mistake people make is to give up on their claim. The second biggest mistake people make is to wait before making their appeal. The appeal process is more complicated than the actual application. So our advice in most cases over the years has been for clients to make the initial application on their own. They may win the case at the outset on just the simple application and not have to get an attorney involved at all. Once a person has been denied social security and is starting the appeal process, it is probably time to consult an attorney.

We get calls in our office on a regular basis from people who have waited weeks after the denial of their initial application before calling. This is a mistake. Once you receive that initial turn down, you should keep your case moving, because if you are sitting on your case, it is likely you are just making a long wait longer. The next chapter is about the long wait that most applicants have to live through between the time of the appeal and the hearing. It is worth emphasizing: the quicker you appeal, the quicker you will get to that hearing.

After the Appeal: The *Long* Wait

After you have been denied your claim and have met with one of our lawyers, our firm will electronically file your appeal. Once the appeal has been filed, the long wait begins. What is happening while you wait? Your claim, along with a request for hearing, will be placed with the Office of Disability Adjudication and Review. A request for a hearing before a social security judge will be filed. There are several different levels regarding any appeal that could warrant special attention from the Social Security Administration. The best possible way to guarantee that your appeal gets the attention it deserves is to work closely with your lawyer and keep him or her updated on your medical status and general condition.

The Social Security Administration is interested primarily in one thing: what proof do you have that you are disabled? Our firm will work closely with you, reviewing all the information you provide via your medical records and medical history and getting this information to the Social Security Administration to provide them with proof of your disability.

If your financial situation worsens along with your medical condition, proof such as bankruptcy filings, eviction notices, unpaid bills, notices of disconnect and repossession can be brought to the attention of the Social Security Administration and request for dire need can be made. This could expedite your case, but these requests are not granted very often.

Needless to say, when you are unable to work and are suffering from an unforeseen debilitating medical condition, you're under a great deal of stress. To make matters worse, often when something like this occurs, the first thing you lose is your medical insurance. This places you in a "catch 22," where you are sick and unable to work and are unable to afford proper medical care. We cannot stress enough how important it is to continue to seek medical care. Even for those without insurance, you'll find that there are different options you can consider, including county facilities, charities and hospitals that will work with an uninsured individual.

Your relationship with your doctor is invaluable in your appeal process. We know the language of the Social Security Administration. If you have a doctor who is supporting you in your claim for disability, we can contact him or her and craft specific letters for your doctor to sign, which could result in an on-the-record decision of your claim. In these cases, it is possible to win without a hearing, but again it is not easy to obtain these decisions.

Be sure to attend all of your doctor's appointments and be diligent with your medical care. This record of your medical treatment is the proof that you are disabled that our law firm provides to the Social Security Administration. Remember that this is the primary information the administration is interested in.

Below are some of the types of information your attorney needs to be made aware of:

1. Visits to a new doctor
2. Emergency room visits
3. New medication and the side effects they cause
4. New diagnosis or new or different medical conditions
5. Mental health: are you suffering from depression? Are you seeing a mental health care provider or being medicated for a mental condition?
6. Are you a veteran who seeks treatment at a VA facility?
7. Have you filed bankruptcy due to your medical bills or inability to work?
8. Have you lost your home or vehicle due to your disability?
9. Do you have a person who is considered your caretaker because you are unable to care for yourself?
10. Are you unable to care for your family and children without assistance?

It is your lawyer's job to provide the proof of your disability to the faceless entity of the Social Security Administration. It is your job as the claimant to help by providing the proper information to your attorney. Your attorney will work to shorten the long wait and, with your help, document the entire process so that you are ready to face the judge when your hearing is scheduled.

My Social Security Hearing

As was noted earlier, many people will eventually have to go through a hearing in order to get their benefits. While the thought of this initially scares most of our clients, it is really nothing to fear because of the following reasons:

1. Social security hearings are usually informal matters; they are hearings, not trials.
2. No one is there to oppose you or cross-examine you as they would at a trial.
3. There are usually only four or five people in the room at the time of the hearing, and you and your lawyer are two of those people.
4. The other people present are usually a judge's assistant and an expert to testify about what jobs you can do.
5. The hearings often are held in small rooms and last on average 30 minutes to an hour.
6. In most cases, you know all the answers to any question that will be asked because you and your life are the subject of the hearing. As we often tell our clients, "You know more about this case than the judge does, because it's all about things that happened to you, not the judge."
7. Most judges are sympathetic to the situation you are in and usually try to make it as easy for you as possible.

As the list above demonstrates, social security hearings aren't like a TV murder trial, with a courtroom of reporters and dueling attorneys. In most cases, it is more in keeping with a polite discussion regarding your situation.

In our practice, we have clients come in and prepare for the hearing before they go to it. We go into a great deal of detail and let you practice a bit so you will not be surprised when you get to the hearing. We think it is important that you feel comfortable at the hearing, while at the same time you are prepared to communicate to the judge in a serious manner all the reasons you are unable to work.

The hearings are informal and should not be stressful, but they are very important and should be taken very seriously, as this is often the place where your case is won or lost.

Part Three: Why I May Need a Lawyer Who Does Both Workers' Compensation and Social Security

Social Security Language and the Workers' Compensation Claim

If you have a workers' compensation injury that is severe and makes you disabled, you should also consider filing for social security benefits with the Social Security Administration. But getting a check for social security benefits and a workman's compensation check at the same time can cause problems. Social Security will want to look at your workers' compensation settlement and may lower your social security benefits after it looks at all your income to determine the amount of benefits you are owed. This is called an offset. The Social Security Administration has rules about how much money you can get while you are collecting a disability check. This is done in order to prevent people from making more money while they are disabled than they did while they were actually working.

The reasoning for this makes sense, and while you won't earn more while you are disabled, you do want to make sure you are getting all that you are entitled to. You want to get the most money possible out of your workers' compensation check and your social security check, and getting lawyers who focus on both areas of the law can be very helpful in this scenario. A knowledgeable workers' compensation attorney will already be looking toward the possibility that a social security claim could be in your future, and for that reason, you may need to put "social security language" in your settlement paperwork and have it approved by a judge. This wording can be made part of your compensation settlement and in some cases get you hundreds or even thousands of extra dollars in social security benefits. If you are going to return to work or have a very small settlement, it is not a necessity that social security language be included in your paperwork, but it something that probably should be included in every case where a worker is clearly never going to return to work and/ or receives a large settlement.

Signing Settlements for Workers' Compensation and Applications for Social Security

Before you sign any workers' compensation settlement paperwork, you should consult a lawyer, as it may cause problems on your social security claim. It is also important for people who file for social security to understand that what they list on their social security claim could also have an impact on their workers' compensation claim. If you file with Social Security and list a number of issues that are unrelated to your compensation case, the workers' compensation insurance company will almost certainly use this against you to show your disability is not from your compensation claim. How to approach this gets very complicated and should be discussed with a lawyer. You want to truthfully provide the information to both the insurance company and Social

Security, but you want to do so in a manner that protects your rights.

These are just a few of the complications that come up when you have both a workers' compensation and a social security claim. Many people don't even know they will have a social security claim when they first get injured at work, and so they don't consider the implications for social security benefits at that time. These matters are often confusing to lawyers and even judges. If you think you might need surgery for you workers' compensation injury, you may want to think about calling an attorney as this is often a sign that these issues may arise in your case.

When deciding to hire a lawyer for a disability claim, you should consider that attorney's general knowledge of disability law. Workers' compensation and social security are very much related. Since we do both at our firm, we are able to make arguments regarding ability to work using two separate areas of the law. We use arguments from social security law in workers' compensation cases and arguments from workers' compensation evaluations in social security hearings

Knowledge of both areas of the law doesn't provide just a strategic advantage. It also can be critical to getting you all the money and benefits you are entitled to. Part Four is a discussion of the various ways having a disability attorney can protect all your rights.

Workers Who Are Specialists or Have Few Skills

Another issue to consider is that many people specialize in a type of work where a single injury may keep them from ever working again. This is often the time where a workers' compensation claim becomes a social security claim. If you have done just one job or one kind of job for your entire life, you may be considered a specialist, and even though the injury might not keep others from returning to work, it may be the kind of injury that puts you on social security. If you have heard the insurance adjuster say "The doctor has put you at MMI" or "You need to have an FCE done" or "We are sending you for a vocational evaluation," you may need to consider hiring a lawyer who does both social security and workers' compensation, because this means the insurance company is already evaluating your ability to return to work. If you have done only one type of work, the insurance company will act as if there are plenty of other jobs you could do even if you have never done them before. A person in this situation needs to look at all their job and disability options carefully.

Medicare

Whether you were hurt at a construction site or you were a nurse lifting a patient, you may end up making an application for social security benefits. If you handle your workers' compensation case by yourself, you may encounter problems with Medicare. Nowadays, it is common for almost every injured worker to be asked by the insurance company about the possibility of closing out medical benefits. Closing out medical benefits in an Alabama workers' compensation case without consulting a lawyer is very dangerous, as it may prevent you from receiving Medicare benefits in the future. Many people do not have a lawyer present at their workers' compensation settlement, and they do not understand all that is at risk when they go to a hearing to close out medical or other benefits. This can be a very tricky decision that, in some cases, can jeopardize your access to future healthcare coverage.

A Special Note on Workers' Compensation Truck and Car Accidents

Over the years we have handled many claims that involve both workers' compensation and auto insurance. These cases can be particularly confusing when it comes to how your personal insurance interplays with the insurance of your employer. If you were in a car or truck accident while you were on the job or you were hit by someone who was driving while he or she was on the job, you should consult a lawyer, as these can be particularly confusing cases. If you were not on the job when you were hit, but the other driver was, you still should consider calling someone with experience in both workers' compensation and car accidents.

Conclusion

In handling hundreds of disability cases, we have learned that it is very difficult for hard working individuals to suddenly find themselves injured and facing an uncertain future. Matters become worse when the worker discovers that quick relief is unlikely and that either their employer or the federal government is challenging their claim. Many of these cases begin with small injuries where the worker was certain that he or she would return to work in a matter of days. Most of these same people were also certain that they would not suffer any long term employment problems. As we have discussed, the inability to return to work is a problem that is far more common than one may think.

If you are hurt at work, or are no longer able to work due to a mental or physical disability, you should take steps to protect yourself now. The fact that you have read even part of this book indicates that you are concerned about your own welfare and the welfare of those you love. If you have applied for social security or workers' compensation, you are right to have these concerns, as there can be surprises in store for you even after you think you have resolved your claim.

It is our hope that we have provided you with some insight into the problems that you are likely to face, in the unfortunate event you are one of those who have to file your Alabama disability claim.

Part Four: Disability Odds and Ends

Five Things People Don't Know about Social Security Cases

1. If you are disabled for one year or more, you may be entitled to benefits even if later you return to work. This is referred to as a closed-period case.
2. Your workers' compensation claim may end up having a significant impact on what you can receive from social security. This is why it is a good idea to consult someone who does both workers' compensation and social security.
3. It is possible to earn small amounts of money and keep your benefits. Social Security allows this to encourage people to test the waters to see if they might return to full-duty work.
4. Large numbers of truly disabled people are denied their claims every year. Most of those people win their cases only after they go to a hearing before a social security judge.
5. Most of the time you are not told whether you have won or lost a hearing at the hearing. You must wait for a decision from the judge.

Five Things People Don't Know About Alabama Workers' Compensation Law

1. The law places a variety of caps and limits on the amount of money you can recover.
2. There are various ways to determine the amount a worker is owed in any given case, and often the insurance company will present you with the very lowest calculation while not explaining other methods by which a higher settlement can be determined.
3. "Pain and suffering" is usually not a factor in determining what amount of money is owed in a workers' compensation case. While pain can be an important component in determining your overall level of disability, it is not considered in the same way it is in other injury cases.
4. You are not entitled to a trial by jury for a workers' compensation injury. Trials are before a judge only.
5. While a fairly large number of workers settle their cases without an attorney, an employer will almost never settle a case without an attorney representing the company. The employer's attorney is not your attorney and cannot look out for your interest. Your employer will never represent themselves in a workers' compensation case. If it is important enough for him or her to pay an attorney, you should seriously consider hiring one yourself.

Five Mistakes Injured Workers Make When They Don't Have a Lawyer

1. *Giving a recorded statement and signing medical releases.* You do not have to do either one in order to file your claim. Usually these are both requested in order to help build a case against you. It is almost never a good idea to do

either of these as they are almost always used to hurt your claim.

2. *Choosing a doctor from a Panel of Four without expert help.* An experienced lawyer knows who the best workers' compensation doctors are, and we can direct you to them. People often will choose the worst comp doctor on the list because the doctor is close to their house or they are familiar with the part of town where the doctor's office is located.
3. *Settling their case and closing out benefits they were not paid to close out.* Alabama Courts have said that general release language may close out benefits that are not explicitly listed as being closed out. This means most people who represent themselves are often giving up rights that are not even listed in the settlement agreement. The Alabama Supreme Court has said it is not necessary for these rights to be listed with specificity.
4. *Closing medical benefits without understanding how this will affect their private insurance or Medicare.* An agreement to close out medical benefits is a significant decision that should not be entered into without legal counsel.
5. *Talking to case managers about their case.* Nurse case managers, as a general rule, are nothing more than spies and advocates for the insurance company. The information you give them can and will be used against you in a court of law. Helpful case managers do exist, but they are, very, very, rare.

Suggestions for Choosing Your Lawyer

1. Choose a lawyer who will actually meet with you on your first visit. You should expect to meet and talk with the lawyer who will handle your case in person and not just talk to him or her over the phone or simply meet with his or her staff.

2. Choose a lawyer you feel personally comfortable with. This can be done only if you have followed suggestion number 1 above.
3. Choose a lawyer who is knowledgeable about disability work.
4. Choose a lawyer who personally explains the process to you.
5. Ask the lawyer you meet with if he or she will be the lawyer who actually works on your case and go to your trial/hearing.

Glossary of Disability Terms and Acronyms

Note: Parenthetical notations indicate in which type of claim the term is most commonly encountered.

wc = workers' compensation

ss = social security

Answer The legal document that the employer/insurance company must file in order to get your lawsuit moving. Not everyone will have a lawsuit, but those who do should know this term, because waiting for the defendant to answer often delays a claim. (wc)

Complaint The initial filing that starts a lawsuit. Usually the worker will file this through his attorney, and the defendant will file a response. In some cases the defendant might actually initiate the suit. (wc)

Deposition A recorded meeting between you, your lawyer and the lawyer for the defendant. The lawyer is able to ask you questions on a wide variety of topics so they can prepare their case. (wc)

Discovery The process by which each side gets to ask the other for information pertaining to the case. (wc)

DOT The Dictionary of Occupational Titles. This is government publication that is considered outdated but is still used in social security hearings to assist in answering questions about jobs and the requirements for those various jobs. (wc and ss)

FCE Functional capacity evaluation. This is a test that is administered to see what work capacity a person has after an accident. These evaluations are somewhat controversial. (wc and ss)

Interrogatories Written questions each side asks of the other once a suit is filed. (wc)

MMI Maximum medical improvement. This is when the doctor thinks that he or she has treated you to the point where you are not likely to experience any more substantial improvements in your condition in the near future. (wc)

Mediation A meeting whereupon the parties attempt to settle their case outside of court. (wc)

Panel of Four A list of four doctors that is provided to you and your attorney by which you can change doctors. This can be one of the most important selections you make in your entire case. (wc)

PT Permanent total. This is jargon used by attorneys to describe a person who is, for all intents and purposes, not going to work again. PT does not mean someone who is totally helpless or totally unemployable. (wc)

TTD Temporary total disability. This refers to the period of time when someone is temporarily unable to work. A check is paid in these situations as long as a workers' compensation physician has noted that the person is incapable of working for reasons related to a compensable workers' compensation injury. (wc)

VE This can refer to a vocational expert or to a vocational evaluation, which is the evaluation performed by such an expert. These experts determine what jobs you are capable of doing after your workers' compensation injury. A vocational expert will almost certainly be present at your social security hearing. (wc and ss)

Questions You May Be Asked

What follows are two brief sets of questions that are typical of questions and topics our clients are asked about in workers' compensation and social security cases. These sets cover the main subjects of questions and topics that are usually asked, but they are just an outline. Questioning regarding medical treatment, doctors visits and therapy may last for well over an hour in both workers' compensation and social security cases. If you look at both sets of questions, you will see that the issues in both cases are very similar and that preparation for one often will help you prepare for the other.

While the lists are similar, the approach to preparation may be radically different. A person preparing for a deposition is often asked to limit the length of the answers as much as possible, but in a social security hearing claimants are often encouraged by the judge and their own attorney to expand on many of their answers in great detail.

It is important to discuss these issues with your attorney before you prepare for a deposition or a hearing.

Basic Questions You May Be Asked at Your Workers' Compensation Deposition

- Would you please state your full name?
- How old are you today?
- What is the highest level of education you have completed?
- What jobs have you held in the past?
- How much were you paid at each of those jobs?
- Why did you leave each job?
- What happened on the day you were injured in this case?
- What medical treatment did you have for this injury?
- Did you recover fully?

- Did your injury extend into other parts of your body?
- Did the workers' compensation doctor give you restrictions?
- Did the workers' compensation doctor give you an impairment rating?
- Have you had a functional capacity evaluation?
- What problems do you still have now?
- How has this injury affected your life?
- What is your average day like?
- Are you taking medications?
- What are their side effects?
- Have you ever been arrested or convicted of a crime?

Basic Questions You May Be Asked at Your Social Security Hearing

- Would you please state your full name?
- How old are you today?
- What is the highest level of education you have completed?
- What jobs have you held in the past?
- Why did you leave your last job?
- Did you quit or get fired due to your disabling condition(s)?
- Have you worked since that day?
- What day did you become disabled?
- What medical treatment do you receive for this condition(s)?
- What problems do you have now?
- How has this injury affected your life?
- What is your average day like?
- Do you suffer from pain?
- Are you taking medications?
- What are their side effects?
- Please rate that pain on a scale of 1–10, with 10 being the worst.
- Do you have anything else that you would like to inform the court?

Part Five: About the Authors

Powell and Denny Law Firm

Powell and Denny was established in 1998 by William Powell and Gregory Denny. The firm has offices in Birmingham and Huntsville, Alabama, but has handled cases in every corner of the state. The lawyers at Powell and Denny practice almost exclusively in the area of Alabama workers' compensation and social security disability but also have a wide variety of legal experience, having tried many jury trials and appealed a wide variety of personal injury matters. Both William Powell and Gregory Denny are graduates of Cumberland School of Law and the National College of Advocacy.

An Interview with William Powell

Why did you become a disability lawyer?

I grew up in Tennessee with a large extended family in Alabama. I had several relatives with serious physical and mental disabilities, and I learned firsthand how devastating a disability can be for the whole family. Part of the reason I am an attorney is because I grew up wanting to help people with disabilities.

How did you meet Mr. Denny?

Greg and I were both young attorneys employed at a law firm with one of the largest practices of social security disability law in the state of Alabama. After several years of practicing together, we decided to leave together and start our own small firm focusing on disability and workers' compensation cases.

What do you like best about handling social security cases?

It's nice to be there when you hear the judge give your client a favorable decision. You spend a lot of time getting to know a person during a traumatic time in their life. It's rewarding to be able to help ease a person's stress during this period.

What surprises people the most about Alabama Workers' Compensation Law?

The limitations in place restricting the amount of compensation they are entitled to for their on-the-job injuries. Most people believe that the sky is the limit when it comes to filing a law suit, but the fact of the matter is, in Alabama there is a cap in effect that limits recovery based upon specific injuries to the body. Injured workers are not entitled to pain and suffering or mental anguish, and this can be very upsetting to the worker. Our job is to help the client maximize his or her recovery to every extent possible.

How did your firm end up handling both types of cases?

Both workers' compensation and social security disability claims deal with people who are currently disabled and unable to work. These types of cases are similar for that reason, and it was a natural progression to handle both types of these cases. Unlike a lot of other disability law firms, our lawyers also have experience doing other complex forms of law work. Both Mr. Denny and I have handled wrongful death cases, 18-wheeler truck accidents and medical malpractice trials. Although we now focus on disability, the work we have done in tough jury trial settings has given us experience in high-pressure courtroom situations.

What is the philosophy of the firm?

To treat our clients with respect. To remain personable with each case so that the client does not feel like he or she is just another file. Basically, to treat the client like we would like to be treated ourselves.

How did you come to write this book?

This book is a way to get information out to people about the basics of social security and workers' compensation law. Having practiced in this area for 20 years, we know what questions are most commonly asked. This book hopefully answers some of those questions.

What do you do with your personal time?

I am married and the father of two young boys. My personal time is spent being a dad. I also am very active with my faith and church, and I volunteer for the Special Needs Program there.

An Interview with Gregory Denny

A version of this interview appeared in winter 2007 in the magazine of the Alabama Association for Justice as part of the Champions of Justice Series.

Greg Denny began defending workers who were injured on the job because he wanted to represent people like his own family.

"I began practicing workers' compensation as soon as I got out of law school," Denny said. "I never could imagine representing someone other than someone like my parents.

"My dad is in the electrical supply industry, and he has never had a workers' comp claim, but he could," Denny said. "Like I said, I try to represent people who are like my relatives, and none of them owned businesses."

Denny, who is former chairman of the Alabama Trial Lawyers Workers' Compensation Division, said about 60 to 70% of his practice is representing injured workers. He said they are very rewarding because you know you are helping someone who cannot help themselves. Denny cites a case in Cullman where a woman had lost her arm and said that, while he was representing her, he became friends with her family.

"After we won the case, we all went out to lunch," he said. "It gives you a good feeling."

Denny, with the help of several other lawyers, started the workers' compensation division two years ago. It currently has its own list serve, holds meetings in conjunction with and separate from ATLA seminars and is working to develop its own board.

"It has been growing pretty consistently," said Denny. "Most of the people who practice workers' comp are in small firms with one or two, maybe three or four, lawyers.

In the last two years, the workers' compensation division's separate seminars have drawn dozens of lawyers from across the state, Denny said. The group currently is planning a third meeting, but the date has not been determined.

"Our long-term goal is to keep everything going for years to come," he said.

One of the group's short-term goals is to work with the Alabama State Bar and other interested entities to reform the state's workers' compensation laws.

Denny pointed out that the payment cap for a permanent injury is woefully low. In fact, if Congress raises the minimum wage to $7 an hour, a healthy worker would earn $280 a week. A person who has lost an eye in a workplace accident, under the current law, would receive only $220 a week—or $60 less than the minimum wage worker. The payments have not been increased in almost two decades.

"That is just not right, it is not fair, and it is something we have to address," he said.

In addition to workers' compensation issues, the division also is promoting charitable causes, especially the Susan G. Komen Foundation and other cancer-related groups.

"Several of the section's most active members have been affected, directly or indirectly, by cancer, and the group has a special awareness of the pain this disease can cause," Denny said.

While he has devoted his law practice to representing injured workers, Denny has enjoyed several "trivial" pursuits. He has appeared on *Jeopardy!* and *Who Wants to Be a Millionaire?*

How did a workers' compensation lawyer who was reared in Jefferson County make it into show business? It is an interesting story.

He and his wife began the habit of watching *Jeopardy!* every night.

"As we watched, my wife commented that I knew a lot of the answers, so I went to Atlanta, took the test and passed, and we went out to Los Angeles to do the show," he said. "I did fairly well but lost to a Harvard law student."

A few months later, he was on *Who Wants to Be a Millionaire?*

Denny also uses his spare time to serve as chair of the advisory committee of the University of Alabama at Birmingham's Philosophy Department, which is a nationally recognized program.

Greg Denny may not have been a *Jeopardy!* champion, but he has made a difference in the lives of hundreds of injured workers, and for that, he is a "Champion of Justice."

Attorney CVs
William V. Powell, Jr.
Partner

phone 256-705-3510 (Huntsville)
205-978-2051
800-227-0882 (toll-free)
fax 205-978-2054
email williampowell@bellsouth.net

William V. Powell, Jr. graduated from the University of Alabama in 1989 and is a 1992 graduate of Cumberland School of Law. He was admitted to the Alabama State Bar in September of 1992 and to the Tennessee State Bar in March 1994. Mr. Powell also has been admitted to the U.S District Court for the Northern District of Alabama and the United States Court of Appeals for the Eleventh Circuit. Mr. Powell's primary areas of focus have been in the field of Workers' Compensation, Social Security Disability, SSI and claims for Personal Injuries. Mr. Powell is currently the chair of the Birmingham Bar's Workers' Compensation section, past chair of the Alabama Association for Justice work Workers' Compensation section, a member of the Alabama Workers' Compensation Organization (AWCO), a member in the National Organization of Social Security Representatives (NOSSCR), a member of the Alabama and Tennessee State Bar Associations, a member of the Birmingham Bar Association, a member of the Alabama Association for Justice, a member of the Alabama Civil Justice Foundation, a member of the Tom Robinson Society Workers' Compensation Group and a member of the Alabama State Bar Workers' Compensation Section. Mr. Powell has been certified as an "Advocate" by the Association of Trial Lawyers of America and has spoken at various seminars on issues dealing with Alabama's Workers' Compensation law.

Areas of Practice:

45% Workers' Compensation
45% Social Security Disability
10% Personal Injury

Litigation Percentage:

60% of Practice Devoted to Litigation

Bar Admissions:

Alabama, 1992
Tennessee, 1994
U.S. District Court Northern District of Alabama, 1992
U.S. Court of Appeals 11th Circuit, 1994

Education:

Cumberland School of Law, Samford University, Birmingham, Alabama, 1992 J.D.

University of Alabama, Tuscaloosa, Alabama, 1989 B.A.
Honors: Dean's List
Major: Political Science

Representative Cases:

Crownson v. Woolard Brothers, Inc., 915 So.2d 1186 (Ala. Civ. App. 2004)

Davis Plumbing Company, Inc. v. Burns, 967 So.2d 94 (Ala. Civ. App. 2007)

Classes/Seminars Taught:

Workers' Compensation Seminar, Alabama Association for Justice, 2004–2007

Workers' Compensation: Tools of the Trade, ABI/CLE, 2007

Birmingham Bar Workers' Compensation Section Judges' Seminar

Honors and Awards:

Named an Advocate by the American Trial Lawyers' Association, 1995–Present

Professional Associations and Memberships:

Alabama State Bar Association, 1992–Present, Member
Tennessee State Bar Association, 1994–Present, Member
American Bar Association
Alabama Association for Justice
Alabama Civil Justice Foundation
Alabama State Bar, Workers' Compensation Section
Birmingham Bar Association
Birmingham Bar, Worker' Compensation Section, Officer
Tom Robinson Society Workers' Compensation Group
Alabama Workers' Compensation Organization (AWCO)
National Organization of Social Security Claims Representatives (NOSSCR)

Gregory Denny
Partner
phone 205-978-2051(Birmingham)
800-227-0882 (toll-free)
fax 205-978-2054
email gregdenny@bellsouth.net

GREGORY DENNY earned his B.A. at the University of Alabama in Birmingham 1988, where he majored in both philosophy and political science. He obtained his J.D. from Cumberland School of Law in 1991. He has served as Chair of both the AAJ Workers' Compensation section and the Birmingham Bar Workers' Compensation section. He has successfully handled hundreds of social security and workers' compensation cases and has worked on these types of cases for twenty years. Mr. Denny began his career studying workers' compensation in law school under Judge Haley and then working in a law firm that did large amounts of social security work.

Mr. Denny is a founding member of Powell and Denny, P.C., where his practice is concentrated in the areas of workers' compensation, social security disability and work-related automobile litigation. Mr. Denny has written articles and organized several conferences on Alabama Workers' Compensation law. He is also one of the founding members of the Tom Robinson Society, a group comprised of more than 30 Alabama lawyers dedicated to fighting for the rights of Alabama's workers. In his spare time, he is the chair of the U.A.B. Philosophy Department's Advisory Committee and has appeared on the game shows *Jeopardy!* and *Who Wants to Be a Millionaire?*

Areas of Practice:

Workers' Compensation
Social Security Disability
Car Accidents

Litigation Percentage:

60% of Practice Devoted to Litigation

Bar Admissions:

Alabama, 1991
U.S. District Court Northern District of Alabama, 1992

Education:

Cumberland School of Law, Samford University, Birmingham, Alabama, 1991 J.D.

University of Alabama at Birmingham, Birmingham, Alabama, 1988 B.A.

Honors: Cum Laude

Honors: Outstanding Student Award 1987–1988

Major: Philosophy/Political Science

Published Works:

"The American Association for Justice Workers' Compensation Initiative," *American Association for Justice Journal*, Winter, 2005

Workers' Compensation (Various Articles etc.), *AAJ*, 2005

Classes/Seminars Taught:

Chair and Speaker, Workers' Compensation from the Plaintiffs Perspective, American Association for Justice, 2005

Chair, Workers Compensation Symposium, American Association for Justice, 2006

Chair and Speaker, "Demystifying Impairments: FCE's, Vocational Reports and the A.M.A. Guidelines," 2007

Speaker, "Dealing with the Large Workers' Compensation Defense Firm," American Association for Justice Mid Winter Conference, 2006

Workers' Compensation: The Plaintiff's Perspective, AAJ, 2005–2007

Workers' Compensation: Dealing with the Large Defense Firm, AAJ, 2006

Honors and Awards:

Alabama Association of Justice "Champion of Justice," 2006–2007

BV Rating by Martindale Hubbell

Professional Associations and Memberships:

Birmingham Bar Workers' Compensation Section, 2006–2007, Chair

AAJ Workers' Compensation Section, 2005–2007, Chair

Birmingham Bar, 2007–2008, Member, Executive Committee

Alabama Association of Justice, Alabama Workers' Compensation Division, 2005–2007, Chair

Tom Robinson Society: A Birmingham Workers' Compensation Group, 2005–Present, Chair

Alabama State Bar, Alabama Workers' Compensation Section, Member

Workers Injury Law & Advocacy Group, www.WILG.org, Member

Pro Bono Activities:

University of Alabama at Birmingham Philosophy Department Advisory Committee, 2003–Present, Chair

For More Information

Visit us online at www.powellanddenny.com and read our blog, Birmingham Workers' Compensation Blog, where we discuss a wide variety of issues relevant to anyone interested in both Alabama workers' compensation and social security matters.

If you've found the information in this book helpful, please visit us on **Facebook** at **Powell and Denny: My Alabama Disability Lawyers**.

You can also follow us on **Twitter: @PowellandDenny**

Acknowledgments

Our legal assistant, Dana Oliver, is essential to our everyday operations and continued success. Her work on this book (not to mention hundreds of workers' compensation and social security cases) has been invaluable.

39251324R00037

Made in the USA
Lexington, KY
14 February 2015